## PRAISE FOR M. B. GOFFSTEIN

"Goffstein is a minimalist, but her text and pictures carry the same emotional freight as William Blake's admonishment to see the world in a grain of sand and eternity in an hour."

—*Time* magazine

"M. B. Goffstein is one of the finest illustrator/writers of our time. Like porcelain, there is more to her work than meets the eye. Beneath the delicacy and fragility is a core of astounding strength."

—*Washington Post*

"A book by M. B. Goffstein is a beautifully simple and simply beautiful thing."

—*New York Times Book Review*

"One of the few modern author-illustrators who are assured classic status."

—*Publishers Weekly*

"It's good to have a Goffstein! She unearths the treasure of simplicity."

—*New York Times Book Review*

# THE COLLECTED WRITINGS OF M. B. GOFFSTEIN

*Words Alone: Twenty-Six Books Without Pictures*

*Art Girls Together: Two Novels*

*Daisy Summerfield's Art: The Complete Flea Market Mysteries*

*Biography of Miss Go Chi: Novelettos & Poems*

# WORDS
# ALONE

M. B. Goffstein

# WORDS ALONE

## Twenty-Six Books Without Pictures

DAVID ALLENDER PUBLISHER

DAVID ALLENDER PUBLISHER
is devoted to the work of author-artist
M. B. Goffstein (1940–2017).

*W. Somerset Maugham wrote that people aren't*
  *always born at home.*
*We can see the world through books, and the*
  *books will be our tents.*

—M. B. GOFFSTEIN, 1986

# CONTENTS

# The Gats!

*The lordly and isolate Satyrs—look at them come in on the left side of the beach like a motorcycle club!*

— CHARLES OLSON

The gats!
Look at them come over the sand
looking for a home
and the fattest gat, their leader,
is dancing the gamba.

They are coming over the sand
looking up
and looking down
and the handsomest gat,
who wears a cravat,
is looking around.

They keep coming across the sand
looking for a home
and the littlest gat, the baby,
trips and falls flat.

"A tree root," says the smartest gat,
who is wearing a hat.
"Imagine that," says the fattest gat,
who is still gamba-ing.

"A tree trunk in the air,"
says the handsomest gat,
looking around.

"Leaves and branches in the sky,"
says the littlest gat,
lying flat on his back.

"A tree, in fact,"
says the smartest gat
from under his hat—
"A gat could live in that."

So they all climb up
to the top of the tree.

The strongest gat,
who carries the vat,
makes soup
and the dumbest gat stirs it
with his baseball bat.

Then all of the gats dance the gamba
balancing soup bowls on their heads
while the tree creaks

and shakes

and finally breaks

and comes down—

Glump.

And the gats go back across the sand
looking for a home.

# Sleepy People

Sleepy people live
wherever there is room
for a little bed.

There may be a family of sleepy people
living in one of your old bedroom slippers,
where they are very cozy
in their warm nightshirts
and night hats.

They yawn.
Ah-ah-ah-aaaaaaaah.

They stretch.
En-en-en-eeeeeeeen.

They smile.
M-m-m-mmmmmmmm.

They are always very sleepy.

Every evening the sleepy father
goes to find cocoa and cookies
for a little bedtime snack.

And the children's eyes are closing
as they chew the cookies
and drink their cocoa
from warm cups.

Then while the sleepy father
snores softly
the sleepy mother
sings to her children
a little song.

"Asleep, asleep, the moon's asleep
in a soft gray cloud,
Asleep, asleep, the sky's asleep
under starry puff,
Asleep, asleep, the bird's asleep
in his small warm nest,
Asleep, asleep, my children sleep
in their own good beds."

Zzzzzzzzzzzz.

# Brookie and Her Lamb

Brookie had a little lamb
and she loved him very much.

Brookie taught the lamb to sing
and he had a very good voice,
but all he could sing was
     Baa baa baa
so she taught him how to read,
and all he could read was
     Baa baa baa
but she loved him anyhow.

Brookie took the lamb for a walk
and a little dog barked at them.

The lamb ate some flowers in the park
and they came home again.

Then Brookie made the lamb a room
with straw and pillows on the floor.

She gave the lamb a music book
with songs that he could sing,
and all the songs said
     Baa baa baa
so he sang them very well.

She made the lamb a cozy place
where he could sit and read
and all his books said
    Baa baa baa
so he liked them very much.

Brookie loved her little lamb
and she scratched him behind his ears.
The little lamb said
    Baa baa baa
and snuggled close to her.

# Across the Sea

# ACROSS THE SEA

Across the sea,
old men sit in doorways
on sun-warmed benches,
intent on their knives,
carving from blocks of wood
small figures
that come to life.

I wish I knew where
an old man sat carving,
and I could sit at his knee
to watch while he whittled
and hear a good story
and know he was making
a good friend for me.

# SOPHIE'S PICNIC

Before the sun came up
Sophie cut a thick wedge of cheese,
a large slice of sausage,
broke off half a loaf of bread,
picked a hard green pear,
and pushed them all into a hole
in the hem of her long full skirt.

She filled a jar with water
and put a lettuce leaf inside it.
She wrapped the jar in one kerchief,
put another on her head,
stepped into her wooden sabots
and walked, clap, clap, clap,
until the sun was high above her
and she came to a sweet field of grass.

Then Sophie felt around the bottom of her skirt
and worked her lunch through the hole in the hem.
She sat down and laid it all out in her lap.

Then she began:
she took a little bite of sausage
then a big bite of bread,
a little bite of sausage

and a big bite of bread,
until she had finished them up.

Then Sophie unwrapped the jar of water,
unscrewed the top,
and took a nice long drink.
She fished out the lettuce leaf
and ate it to clean out her mouth.

She had a bite of pear
with a bite of cheese,
a bite of pear
with a bite of cheese,
and when they were gone
Sophie took another long swallow of water,
then lay down, smiling at the sun.

After a while she sat up
and got a small square of chocolate
out of her jacket pocket.
She took tiny bites
and drank some water.

When every speck was gone
Sophie wrapped the jar up
and walked home, clap, clap, clap,
before the sun went down.

## ON THIS DAY

On this day
I'm going to pick
a big bouquet
and put it in my shoe
and let it sail away.
And when it gets
across the sea,
how amazed
the children there
will be!

# Goldie the Dollmaker

Goldie Rosenzweig's parents were dead, so she lived alone in their house and went on with her father's work of carving small wooden dolls and her mother's work of painting bright clothes and friendly faces on them. In four years she had carved, painted, and sold as many dolls as her parents used to do in eight, and there were always more orders for her dolls than she could fill.

• • •

Goldie Rosenzweig fought hard and quietly to get a new doll's face free from the bit of wood that was smothering it, and once she had carved the head and body, she could not lay it down on the worktable and go to bed. She felt responsible for the little wooden person who would not exist but for her, so she went through the wood basket until she found four sticks of wood that really looked as if they wanted to make arms and legs for the new doll.

She laid them on the table and tucked the doll into her pocket while she made herself some dinner. Then Goldie stayed up all night, measuring and carving a little pair of arms with hands and a little pair of legs with shoes on their feet.

When she put the doll together with pins that would allow its arms and legs to be moved, the sun was shining and Goldie went to bed. Her own joints felt much stiffer than the doll's.

GOLDIE WOKE up at noon and thought of the new doll at once. She got right out of bed and sat down at the worktable and looked at the doll for a long time. Then she reached for her knife and sat in her night-gown until late afternoon, absorbed in the careful work of making the new doll as nice to look at and as agreeable and cozy to hold as possible. She ate a bun and drank some tea, washed up, and got back to work.

At dusk the little doll was done. Then Goldie swept and cleaned, and when everything was good she washed herself and brushed her hair back, put on a clean nightgown, and sat down by the door. She folded her hands in her lap and thought about the carpenter who made the wooden crates for her dolls.

Omus Hirschbein was handsome and friendly and exactly her age, but it was because he made things out of wood that Goldie often thought about him. She felt that they were alike and should be good friends.


THE NEXT morning Goldie got out her paints and carefully mixed a flesh color for the doll. She covered its face, neck, and ears, its arms and hands with the rosy tan paint, and then waited for it to dry.

As the day went on, Goldie ate buns and drank tea and painted the doll's curls a glossy dark brown. She painted a white camisole and matching knickers on the doll's body, gray stockings on her legs, and pretty black shoes on her feet. Then she painted a little gleaming black eye on either side of the doll's nose, and finally, holding it firmly around the waist with one hand, Goldie smiled and smiled into the doll's eyes in the friendliest, sweetest way, and she painted a smile right back to herself on the little doll's face.

That smile was why shops could not keep Goldie Rosenzweig's dolls in stock, and that smile was why there were more orders for her dolls than she could fill. There was no little girl, no parent, aunt, or un-cle of a little girl anywhere in the world who could see a little wooden doll that smiled with such friendliness and sweetness, and then buy a different doll to take home. They said that if you looked at a Goldie Rosenzweig doll, you bought her, even if you weren't going to buy any doll in the first place. Because the truth about that smile was that it was heartbreaking.

It was the most satisfying thing to hold a little Goldie Rosenzweig doll in your hand and know that she was going to be kissed a lot and taken everywhere, be given the best doll's wardrobe in the world, and be made very happy.

.•.

One day three little wooden dolls sat facing each other for company on the worktable because Goldie Rosenzweig was going out. She pulled on her boots, got into her jacket, and tied a kerchief under her chin. "I am going to get your crate," she said, "and I won't be gone long."

Then she went out the door of her parents' house, walked quickly across a field and slowly through a little forest, where she had the good luck to find enough wood for two more dolls before she came to the carpenter's shop.

"Hello, Goldie," said Omus Hirschbein. "What can I do for you today?"

"I've made three more dolls, and I need another crate."

"That's fine," said Omus. "I can have one ready for you in an hour."

"Oh, thank you! And could you keep this wood for me while I go shopping?"

"Sure, Goldie, but I'd still like to know why you don't ever want to use my wood scraps."

Goldie shook her head. "I just don't like to use pieces of wood that are all clean and square from the saw."

"But your parents always did. It saved them a lot of trouble."

"I remember," said Goldie. "I don't see how they could."

"But what difference does it make?"

"It just doesn't seem as real, so it's not as interesting to carve. And then it doesn't turn out as good. It never looks alive."

Omus pushed back his cap and scratched his head.

"They're just dolls, Goldie."

"I know, but I make them. So to me they're not just dolls. I have to love making them. And besides, to little girls they're not just dolls—"

"All right, all right!" Omus laughed. "I believe you!"

He took Goldie's wood into his shop, and she walked on until she came to the town.

THE SUN was shining on the dancing treetops above the dappled shady street, and Goldie walked along excitedly, looking into all the shops.

In the dim, dusty hardware store she bought a pound of nails and a pot of blue paint from old Mr. Gottesman, who rubbed his plump hands together briskly and beamed at her through his glasses. "Well, well, well," he said. "You do a good business, so I do a good business! Your poor parents never did such a business."

"I don't think they cared about it as much as I do," said Goldie. "Didn't the little pins I ordered come in yet?"

"Of course not!" cried Mr. Gottesman. "That was a special order, and a special order takes time."

"Well, I'll come in again next week," she said, and went out the door and on down the street.

"GOLDIE!" MRS. Stern called from her bakery. "I'll bet you smelled the buns I just took out of the oven."

"Mm-m-m." Goldie came into the shop and sniffed the delicious warm smell. "I certainly do now!" And Mrs. Stern chuckled delightedly.

Just then a little girl walked in, holding a Goldie Rosenzweig doll in her hand. "You can choose anything you want," she was telling it earnestly, "anything at all."

"Rosie," said Mrs. Stern, and she winked at Goldie. "Do you know who—"

"No!" whispered Goldie, shaking her head at Mrs. Stern. Then she stood shyly and proudly, watching the little girl Rosie and her doll until they chose a big round sugar cookie and went out trading bites.

"Wasn't that sweet!" said Mrs. Stern.

Goldie nodded happily. "I just don't like to say that I make the dolls," she apologized. "It just doesn't seem right." She bought a dozen buns and said goodbye to Mrs. Stern. Then she went across the street to her favorite store.


MR. SOLOMON imported beautiful things from all over the world, and he sold as many of Goldie Rosenzweig's dolls as he could get. He rose as she came into his gloomy, fragrant shop. "Well, Goldie, have you brought me any dolls today?"

"No, but I will next week," she promised. "I just came in now to buy some tea."

"I've got a new kind that I think you will like," he said, but Goldie didn't hear him. An exquisite little lamp had caught her eye, and she was kneeling in front of the low table it stood on.

"Ah," said Mr. Solomon. "That little Chinese lamp."

"Oh-h, it's lovely," breathed Goldie, stroking the fragile porcelain globe with her finger.

"You have good taste." Mr. Solomon smiled and his gold tooth shone. "I'm glad you could see it before I sent it away."

"Why? Has someone bought it? Has it been sold?" Goldie's throat ached.

"Who would buy it?" he asked. "It is such a small thing for so much money. No one would buy it."

Goldie touched the gleaming china base, examined the little carved wooden stand, and looked up at Mr. Solomon.

"So I am sending it to my brother's store," he continued. "He has wealthy customers who appreciate good things." And shaking his head sadly over his own customers, Mr. Solomon went to the back of the store to measure out the tea.

Goldie stayed with the little lamp. "Mr. Solomon," she said when he came back with her tea, "if I sold twenty-seven of my dolls, I could buy it."

"You want to buy this little lamp?"

"It's the most beautiful thing I've ever seen," she said.

"Well," said Mr. Solomon. "Well, just let me think for a minute."

Goldie stood up and looked around the store without much interest, while Mr. Solomon tapped his gold tooth with a pencil.

"Miss Rosenzweig," he said at last, "since you and I do business together, I can give you a special price on the lamp."

"Oh, thank you very much!"

Mr. Solomon held up his hand for silence. "Also," he said, "you save me the trouble of sending it to my brother. And"—he pointed at the lamp—"you appreciate it."

"Oh, yes!"

"So I'll take off one-third of the price for you, and you can take it home with you now."

"But it will take me three months to make eighteen dolls," said Goldie.

"Of course," said Mr. Solomon. "Meanwhile, you can enjoy the lamp." He went to find the wooden crate it had come in, and Goldie took out her money to pay for the tea.

But when he came back, Mr. Solomon waved it away. "The tea is a present," he said. "It's not every day I make such a big sale."

•••

I t was already growing dark when, holding the precious crate, Goldie walked carefully through the fallen leaves, back to Omus Hirschbein's shop.

"What have you got there?" he asked her, looking curiously at the Chinese writing on the top of the crate.

"You aren't going to start having your doll crates made in China, are you?"

"Oh, no," Goldie laughed. "I bought something that came from China." She went inside the shop and carefully set it down. "I'll show you what it is," she said, and she lifted the little lamp out of its crate and stood it up on the counter. "Look. Isn't this beautiful?"

"It's cute," said Omus, "but it won't give you much light."

"No, really look at it! See how beautifully it's made and painted."

Omus looked more closely, and he saw the price tag. "Is that what you paid for it?" he asked in a voice filled with horror.

"I am paying one-third less," said Goldie, "and I'm paying for it in dolls. But I would have paid the full price—I would have paid more! It's the most beautiful thing I've ever seen in my life."

"You know, Goldie," Omus said slowly, "I think you must be a real artist."

Goldie flushed with pleasure. "Why?" she asked him. "Why do you think so?"

"Because you're crazy."

"Oh." Goldie tried to smile.

"Here's your doll crate," said Omus, "and I'll put your wood and these little packages inside it so you'll have less to carry."

"Thank you."

Goldie laid the little lamp back in its crate, but all her pleasure in it was gone, and as she walked back to her parents' house in the darkness, through the little forest and over the field, she was planning desperately to return it to Mr. Solomon early the next morning.

She was crazy to have bought it, no matter how beautiful it was. It *wouldn't* give much light, and it had cost so much that she would scarcely be able to eat for three months, until she had paid for it. And she would need more paint, and the little pins to attach the dolls' arms and legs with, and more crates . . .

And Goldie came home at last, feeling scared and sick and lonely. She wandered around inside the dark little house like a stranger, not wanting to sit in any of the chairs or lie down on the bed. And she tried not to look at the wooden crate with the Chinese writing on it lying beside the three little wooden dolls on the worktable in the moonlight.

She felt empty inside, as if she were hollow, but the hollowness ached and pounded, and finally, in a daze, she sat down by the door.

She stayed there for a long time, then she heard herself whisper, "I'm lonely."

"I'm so lonely," she said. Then she cried wearily until at last she fell asleep at her little place by the door.

SHE DREAMED she felt a light tap on her shoulder.

"Please," said a warm, polite voice. "Please!"

"Yes?" said Goldie.

"That lamp you bought."

"Yes?"

"I made it."

"Oh, it's beautiful!" said Goldie.

"So we are friends."

"But I don't know you," she said. "I wish I did."

"You do know me," laughed the voice. "You know me better than the people I see every day."

"But who are you?"

"I made that lamp you bought today!"

"Oh," said Goldie. "Oh! I see." And she sat for a moment, smiling. "But you don't know me," she said suddenly.

"Yes I do. I made the lamp for you—whoever you are."

Goldie laughed and laughed.

"You understand!" cried the voice.

"Yes," said Goldie. "That's the way *I* carve little wooden dolls and paint their clothes and faces on them."

.•.

In the middle of the night, Goldie woke up. She went over to the worktable, lifted the little lamp out of its crate, set it gently down, and lighted it. Then she sat down and examined the scene that was painted on the globe.

A Chinese family was having a picnic by a little stream, beneath a lovely drooping tree. Two children were sailing flowers in the stream while an old man and woman in flowing robes sat on red chairs, watching. Three beautiful ladies knelt on the ground, preparing the dishes of food with slender, dainty fingers, and behind them, on a terrace, a gentle, beautiful man stood smiling. Each lovely line was alive with truth, and the deep, rich colors glowed.

The china base of the lamp was completely different. Wild black-and-white horses galloped and bucked and reared all around it, but their tails and manes made a calm, swirling design. And the black wooden base with its three round feet was simply carved to hold the lamp firmly in place.

Goldie let out her breath with a sigh of pleasure and looked around the room.

After all, it was such a tiny house. The little lamp filled it all with a soft, cozy light.

"My house," Goldie thought for the first time in her life. "My own little house, with my knife and lamp and tea, my bed and worktable and wood, where I make little wooden dolls for friends."

# Two Piano Tuners

Every morning Reuben Weinstock, the piano tuner, got stiffly out of bed, and washed and shaved in hot water at the kitchen sink. Then he went into his bedroom and brushed his thick gray hair, got dressed in a clean shirt and trousers, put his beautiful old maroon wool robe over them, and tying the silky tasseled cord around his waist, went back into the kitchen to start breakfast cooking.

He put water on the stove in a blue-and-white enameled saucepan and an old yellow coffeepot. Then he opened the cupboard and set the table with a blue plate and an orange plate, a navy-blue bowl and a green bowl, plaster salt and pepper shakers that had seashells stuck into them and bright red plastic tops, two white paper napkins, two knives and two spoons with yellow plastic handles, and two big white cups.

Almost everything in the cupboard had been given to Reuben Weinstock two years ago by the ladies whose pianos he tuned, when they heard that his son and daughter-in-law had died in another town and left him their little girl.

"But how can you take her?" Mrs. Perlman had asked him kindly. "You are a widower, Mr. Weinstock, and you are not a young man anymore, either. What can you give her?"

"Well, I know music," he had said. "I know music. I have tuned pianos for all the great pianists, and I used to travel with Isaac Lipman. I can teach the little girl to play the piano, and she might become a great concert artist!"

"Or a piano teacher," agreed Mrs. Perlman.

Almost all the ladies had given him something—dishes, little dresses, a small bed and dresser. "And if you need any advice, please feel free to ask me," every one of them said.

. • .

By the time he finished setting the table, the water on the stove was boiling. Reuben Weinstock gently dropped three brown eggs into the blue-and-white saucepan, measured coffee into the yellow pot, took out a bottle of milk and a dish of butter, and put four slices of bread on the toast rack. Then he slowly went upstairs, holding on to the rail.

There was only one room upstairs, a big low-ceilinged room. When Reuben Weinstock climbed the top step, he was standing right in the middle of the room, looking down at a long little bump under a fuzzy blue blanket.

"Debbie," he whispered. "It's morning, Debbie."

The long bump curled into a round ball under the blanket.

"Wake up, little Debbie!"

"Hm-m-m-m-m," sang the bump. "Hm-m-m-m-m."

"Hm-m-m-m-m," sang Mr. Weinstock, a little bit lower. "Hm-m-m-m-m. I'm afraid you are sharp again this morning, Debbie."

She jumped out of bed in her long pink pajamas and ran downstairs to play middle C on the piano: C! C! "You are right, Grandpa Reuben," she called, and went into the kitchen to wash her face and brush her teeth at the sink.

When she came back upstairs, her bed was made, and Mr. Weinstock, whose back ached from bending over, was laying out her clean clothes on it.

"Oh, no, Grandpa!" cried Debbie. "Not my jumper! Don't you remember that I don't have school today, so I don't have to wear my jumper?"

"I thought you wanted to come with me to the Auditorium to tune the grand piano."

"Of course I do!"

"Would you like to wear a prettier dress?"

"I want to wear pants."

"Not to go with me," said Mr. Weinstock.

"Oh, Grandpa Reuben," stormed Debbie. "I want to *help* you."

"Then put on your jumper," he said, stroking her bushy hair kindly, "and if you can play your piano lesson well this morning, you may carry my black bag into the Auditorium."

"Will the pianist be there?"

"I think so."

"And won't he be amazed to see a little girl coming to tune that piano?"

"He certainly will be," agreed Mr. Weinstock as he began to make his way carefully downstairs.

"If he thinks I tuned the piano, he won't show up for the concert," chuckled Debbie, who had dressed and gotten downstairs at his heels. "He'll be too scared!"

. • .

After breakfast, while Mr. Weinstock cleared the kitchen table, washed the dishes, and swept up the crumbs, Debbie played her piano lesson for him. It was *Reverie*, by Felix Mendelssohn, and she had been playing it for the past three weeks.

Now Mr. Weinstock came in, drying the last dish. "It is still not so good," he said sadly.

Debbie jumped down from the piano stool. "I know it," she said. "We have to tune this old piano again."

She started to raise the lid, but Mr. Weinstock went back into the kitchen to hang up his dish towel, saying, "We must leave for the Auditorium. Get your coat and hat, Debbie—and brush your hair."

Then he went into his bedroom and changed from his robe into the jacket that matched his dark blue pants. He tucked a clean handkerchief into his pocket and helped Debbie on with her coat.

"I'm sorry you played so badly," he said as he tied her hat strings under her chin.

But when they got to the Auditorium, he handed her his black bag anyway, and Debbie proudly carried it inside.

The pianist *was* already there, but he did not even see her. "Reuben!" he cried, and hurried up the aisle, past rows of empty seats, to hug Mr. Weinstock.

"Isaac!" Mr. Weinstock hugged him back.

They kept their hands on each other's shoulders and beamed at each other. "You look well! You look well!" they said.

"But what are you doing here?" asked Mr. Weinstock.

"You were expecting Walter Bernheimer?"

"Yes!"

"I heard from my manager that he couldn't get here, and I decided to surprise you. I have been on the train since yesterday morning, in order to play here this afternoon."

"You! Oh, that's wonderful. Oh, now we'll hear some real music!"

"And I, once again, after all these years, will play on a piano that is perfectly tuned," said the great concert pianist.

He looked down, as if to make sure that Reuben Weinstock had his bag of tuning instruments with him, and he saw Debbie, still holding on to it.

"Who is this?" he asked.

"This is the piano tuner," joked Mr. Weinstock. He put his hand on Debbie's shoulder. "This is my granddaughter, Deborah Weinstock, who came to live with me two years ago."

"And I really *could* tune that piano."

"You could?"

Debbie nodded uncertainly.

"I want her to play the piano, and she always wants to tune or make repairs."

"That kind of work isn't good for a pianist's hands," Isaac Lipman warned her.

Debbie tucked her hand into her grandfather's hand. "Well, I'm going to be a piano tuner," she said.

"Your grandfather is the best piano tuner in the world, you know, so I hope you are taking good care of him."

"I'm going to," said Debbie.

Isaac Lipman put his arm around Mr. Weinstock for a moment. "Now I must go back to the dressing room and rest," he said. "Please come back when you have finished your work, and we'll have a good visit."

They all walked down the aisle together. Isaac Lipman went up onto the stage and disappeared, while Mr. Weinstock and Debbie took off their coats and hats and laid them on two chairs in the front row. Then they took off their overshoes and went up the stairs to the stage.

• • •

M r. Lipman had been practicing before they came, so the grand piano was already open and the top was up. Mr. Weinstock slid out the music rack and carried it to the back of the stage and leaned it up against the wall.

Then he went back to the piano, sat down, adjusted the bench, and played a few notes. He got up again to take off his jacket and hang it over the back of a wooden chair that was standing near the piano, and he rolled up his shirtsleeves.

Debbie had set his bag down on the floor beside the piano bench. Mr. Weinstock knelt down and opened it and took out his tuning hammer and screwdriver, a strip of red felt, and two little gray felt wedges. He took his tuning fork out of its case and put the case back into his bag.

He stood up and laid the red felt strip inside the piano and began to poke it between the strings with his screwdriver. Then he fitted the tuning hammer onto a pin, hit the tuning fork against his knee, touched it to the metal frame, listened, sat down again, and began to tune the grand piano.

C! C! C! he played. C! C! C! And he pushed the hammer a little to the left. C AND C! F AND C! G AND C! G AND D! F AND D! A AND D! He played each interval over and over again, turning the tuning pins one at a time with the tuning hammer, winding the piano strings more tightly or loosening them a little, until each note was pure and beautiful.

F AND A! F AND A! Debbie stood looking into the piano, at the long line of strings, the heavy iron frame, the yellow wood sounding board, and the flat black dampers, and hummed the notes that were being tuned. She was enjoying the feeling she had of being able to sing two notes at a time.

She always knew which notes would come next; she knew the whole tuning pattern by heart. She thought it was beautiful and exciting, and she liked it better than any music she had ever heard.

"Please stop that, Debbie," said Mr. Weinstock. "I can't hear anything when you hum."

Debbie put her hand over her mouth, and Mr. Weinstock went on tuning: A AND E! A AND E! G AND E! E AND B! Then Debbie forgot and started humming again.

"Debbie!"

"I'm sorry, Grandpa."

G AND B! B AND D! G AND B AND D! G AND B AND D! B AND F-SHARP! F-SHARP AND A!

"Debbie?" said Mr. Weinstock.

She looked at him in amazement. "I wasn't humming!"

"No, I just remembered that I'm supposed to tune Mrs. Perlman's piano, too, this morning."

"Oh," said Debbie.

"Would you go over to her house now and ask her if I may do it tomorrow instead?"

"Do I have to go now, before you're through working on this piano?"

"I would like you to, so you'll be back in time to visit with Mr. Lipman."

"But are you going to take out the action?"

Debbie loved to see the long row of hammers, with their thin shanks and workmanlike red and gray and white felt tops, flip up when Mr. Weinstock hit the keys. She liked the files, the grease, the needles, and all of the good little tools her grandfather might use if he took the action out of the piano.

"No," said Mr. Weinstock. "Mr. Lipman didn't say that there was anything wrong, and everything seems fine to me."

"But you might have to change a string."

"I hope not. Anyway, you've seen me do that a hundred times."

"I like it when they break," said Debbie.

"Well, you'll be back long before I'm done!"

So Debbie walked across the front of the stage, down the steps, and over to the seat that held her coat and hat. She put them on, then sat down to buckle her overshoes.

"Can you do everything by yourself?" Mr. Weinstock called from the stage.

"Yuh," said Debbie, holding her hat strings down with her chin while she tried to make a bow.

But Mr. Weinstock came down to help her. "Now, you be sure to tell Mrs. Perlman that Isaac Lipman is here, so she won't miss the concert this afternoon. And ask her if it's all right to tune her piano tomorrow."

"I will."

"Be very careful."

Debbie nodded seriously. She walked up the dim, empty aisle alone, opened the door, and went into the lobby. She took a drink from the drinking fountain, then she pushed open one of the heavy front doors and went outside. It had been snowing just a little, not enough to stick.

She went down the wide gray stone steps to the sidewalk. Two big dogs, one black and one tan, and a little spotted dog stood talking together on the corner. "Hello," thought Debbie. "Hello, dogs, here comes the piano tuner!"

She crossed the street and started up the long block, looking at each house as she passed it: the white one with red shutters, the dark green one with yellow trimming, the pretty little gray house with soft brown bushes in front and a baby looking out the window. "There goes the piano tuner," she thought for the baby.

And she went past Mrs. Perlman's brown house with white lace curtains in the windows. She was going home first!

.•.

Their house was painted yellow, with a dark red roof. It was at the end of the block, behind a grassy, empty lot. Debbie cut through the lot and went in the back door and through the kitchen.

In the living room, next to the piano, was a bureau with a lot of old tuning instruments in its bottom drawer. Debbie sat down on the carpet and pulled the drawer out. She took out the tuning hammer that Reuben Weinstock never used because its handle was too long. It was a little bit rusty, but so was the only tuning fork Debbie could find that said C on it. She found one gray felt wedge and one black rubber one.

Debbie brought them upstairs to her room, put them on the bed, took off her coat, got out of her jumper, stepped into her pants, and put the coat back on. The pants had an elasticized waistband, which was perfect for holding the tuning hammer up inside them, and she put the tuning fork and wedges into her back pocket. She buttoned her coat on the way downstairs and went out the door, back through the vacant lot, and down the block to Mrs. Perlman's house.

She climbed the front steps and pressed the doorbell and waited for a long time. Finally she pressed the bell again.

"Why, Debbie," said Mrs. Perlman, opening the door. "I looked out the window before, but I couldn't see anyone!"

"That's all right," said Debbie.

"Won't you come in?"

"My grandpa says he hopes you don't mind if I tune your piano."

"What?"

"Well, his friend Isaac Lipman came to give a concert, and he says you should come."

"Isaac Lipman came here?"

"He's at the Auditorium, and Grandpa Reuben is tuning the piano for *him* instead of for Walter Bernheimer," Debbie explained.

"Do you mean to say that Isaac Lipman is giving a concert here, this afternoon?"

"Yes, and I have to help my grandpa. He asked me to come and tune your piano."

"Oh, how thrilling!" exclaimed Mrs. Perlman.

"I'll do a good job," said Debbie, taking off her coat on her way over to Mrs. Perlman's little upright piano in the living room.

"But—" said Mrs. Perlman. "Oh, what does it matter?" she thought. "She's too little to hurt anything, and Mr. Weinstock will certainly do it over again, anyway." So she followed Debbie into the living room and began to take the little round lace doilies and candy dishes and china figurines away from the top of the piano.

Debbie put her coat and hat down on a slippery satin chair and took off her overshoes and put them in the hall. Then, when Mrs. Perlman had finished clearing the piano top, she helped Debbie raise the lid and pull off the front panel. They set it carefully down on the carpet and leaned it against the wall.

Debbie pulled the tuning hammer out of her waistband, the tuning fork and wedges out of her pocket, and sat down at the piano, looking at the strings. There were two strings for each note.

She hit the tuning fork against her knee, held it to a part of the metal frame, listened to it carefully, and then tried the piano: C! C! C! C!

"Would you like to have some cookies and a glass of milk, Debbie?"

"Maybe later," Debbie said. She fitted her tuning hammer onto the pin that held the first string for middle C, and put a wedge between the other C string and the first C-sharp string.

She hit the tuning fork against her knee again and held it to the metal frame and listened very, very closely. C! C! she played, and pushed the hammer. C! C! C! C! C! The gray felt wedge fell out, and Debbie put it back. C! C! C! C! C! C! C!

She wished that Mrs. Perlman wouldn't keep standing right beside her.

Luckily, Mrs. Perlman, who had always been a great admirer of Isaac Lipman, felt that she could not wait another minute to decide what to wear to his concert. She patted Debbie on the shoulder and ran upstairs.

• • •

As Reuben Weinstock finished tuning the bass notes on the grand piano in the Auditorium, he thought to himself that Debbie should be back any moment. He moved his tuning hammer and screwdriver up to the top of the piano, pushed wedges between the strings, and started tuning the treble notes.

He kept looking at the door while he worked, and by the time he had finished tuning the treble and testing the whole keyboard up and down, and Debbie still had not come, he felt very, very worried. He put his tools back into his black bag, shut it, and sat back down on the piano bench, with his eyes on the door.

"Reuben," said Isaac Lipman, coming onto the stage behind him, "if only I had known what a comfortable couch there is in the dressing room in this Auditorium, I would have come here before. I had a wonderful sleep!"

Mr. Weinstock turned to look at him but did not smile.

"What's the matter?" asked Isaac Lipman. "Where did that little granddaughter of yours go? I want to hear her play."

Mr. Weinstock stood up. "I sent her to ask one of our neighbors, who lives only a block away from here, if I may tune her piano tomorrow instead of today, because you are here. She should have been back an hour ago."

"She probably stayed there to tune it herself," said Mr. Lipman. "Let me try the piano while we are waiting for her. Then I want to take you both out to lunch."

He sat down and began to play. "Bravo!" he said. "Bravo, Reuben. There are few enough good piano tuners in the world, but there is only one Reuben Weinstock."

But Mr. Weinstock had left the stage and was standing in front of the first row of seats, putting on his coat and hat. "Thank you," he said. His hands were shaking, and he could hardly button his overcoat.

"Are you going out to find the little girl? Just wait a minute and I'll come with you. I think a little walk would be good for me after that nap." And Isaac Lipman went backstage to get his things from the dressing room.

. . .

"She hasn't come back yet? All right, let's go," he said, coming down from the stage wearing his coat and scarf and a black fur hat.

"I'm so sorry this had to happen today, while you are here—and before your concert," Mr. Weinstock said to him as they walked up the aisle. They went through the lobby and outdoors.

"I'm only sorry because of you," said Isaac Lipman. "You don't look well, Reuben. You seem very tired. I'm afraid it has been hard on you, taking care of that little girl."

"She is my son's child," said Mr. Weinstock. "He and his wife died two years ago."

"I'm sorry, Reuben."

"Now Debbie is all I've got," said Mr. Weinstock. "But she is so much!"

The two men walked up the block in silence, looking all around for Debbie or for anyone who might have seen her. A big black dog trotted ahead of them for a while, then he turned off at the house with the baby.

A minute later they came to Mrs. Perlman's house, and Reuben Weinstock stopped. "This is where she was supposed to come," he said.

A AND E! A AND E! A AND E! they heard in the damp air. A AND E! A AND E! A AND E!

. .

"Ah," said Isaac Lipman. "You see, I was right!"

"But how—" began Mr. Weinstock. "But she will ruin the piano!" he said. "She doesn't know how to tune a piano. She has never tuned one before."

"If she has been living with you for two years, then I'm sure she knows how. But Reuben, she is very naughty!"

Mr. Weinstock put his hand on his friend's arm. "Don't say that. Thank God she is safe. Whatever she has done to the piano, I can fix. She probably meant to help me. She always wants to help me!"

"She *should* help you, Reuben."

"She is only a little girl. I don't want her to help me; I have to help her. I am giving her piano lessons—that is all I can give her. But I have been hoping that she will be a concert artist someday."

"When I was her age, I had already played for the empress of Russia," said Isaac Lipman. "Reuben, your little granddaughter may be as talented as I am. But if she doesn't want to be a pianist more than anything else in the world, she will certainly never be one. She says she wants to be a piano tuner, so let's see how well she is tuning that piano." And taking Mr. Weinstock's arm, he marched up the walk to the front door and pressed the bell.

They stood on the top step and listened to Debbie's tuning until Mrs. Perlman opened the door. "Oh!" she gasped.

"Mrs. Perlman, may I present Mr. Isaac Lipman?" said Mr. Weinstock.

"How do you do? I'm so thrilled to meet you! I recognized you from your picture. Do you know I have your autograph? I've kept it for twenty years. Debbie said you were here. She's in the living room, tuning my piano. Come in, come in!"

They wiped their feet on the mat and took off their boots. Then they followed Mrs. Perlman into the living room, wearing their coats and holding their hats.

Debbie was standing between the piano bench and the keyboard, looking impatient and unhappy. "I've only done two octaves," she said.

"You shouldn't have done any," said her grandfather. "You should have come right back to the Auditorium. I was very worried about you."

"Won't you take off your coats and sit down?" Mrs. Perlman was asking.

"Mr. Lipman can't—" began Mr. Weinstock.

But Isaac Lipman took off his coat and scarf and handed them to Mrs. Perlman. "Thank you very much," he said. "I am sorry to trouble you."

"It's not any trouble. It's an honor!" said Mrs. Perlman. "Let me take your coat, Mr. Weinstock."

"Get out of there for a minute," Mr. Lipman said to Debbie, "and let me see if you are doing a good job."

"I've only done two octaves," Debbie repeated, but she took the wedges out of the strings, picked up the tuning hammer, and slid out.

Mr. Lipman sat down and began to play.

"On my piano!" marveled Mrs. Perlman, coming back from hanging up the coats in her hall closet. "Isaac Lipman, playing on my piano!"

Mr. Lipman smiled. "Now, Debbie," he said. "I have traveled all over the world giving concerts, and I have played on pianos tuned by hundreds of different piano tuners—"

"And Grandpa Reuben was the best?" asked Debbie.

"That's right."

"Well, it's very, very hard to get every note dead-on, the way he does," she told him.

"It would be almost impossible with that kind of tuning hammer," said Mr. Weinstock. "It's no good. The handle is too long. I'm surprised you didn't break any strings."

"Then I think she did pretty well!" said Mr. Lipman.

"And what tuning fork did you use?" her grandfather asked her. "This? It's all rusted." He hit it against his shoe and held it to his ear. "It doesn't play a true C anymore, Debbie."

Debbie's eyes filled with tears.

"Come," said Mr. Lipman, getting up from the piano. "I want to take you all out to lunch."

"My husband will be coming home for lunch soon," said Mrs. Perlman. "I've got a big meal ready, so please stay and eat with us."

"Ah," said Isaac Lipman. "A home-cooked meal . . ."

"It would be a great honor to have you."

"Thank you."

"It is very kind of you, Mrs. Perlman," said Reuben Weinstock, "and I am sorry about your piano. I'll come and tune it first thing tomorrow."

Mrs. Perlman put her arm around Debbie. "Please don't say anything more about it," she said.

"And now," said Isaac Lipman, "I would like to hear Debbie play."

"Play the Mendelssohn *Reverie*, Debbie," said Mr. Weinstock. "We will all remember that the piano is out of tune."

Mrs. Perlman and the two men sat down, and Debbie went to the piano.

.•.

"Is there anything you would rather play?" Isaac Lipman asked her when she was done. "Is there any other piece that you like to play better than this one?"

"No," said Debbie.

Mr. Lipman shook his head sadly, smiling at Mr. Weinstock.

"I think she will be a very lovely piano teacher someday," Mrs. Perlman said kindly, getting up to go to the kitchen.

"The world would be a better place if people who did not like to play the piano did not teach the piano," said Mr. Lipman. "Everybody should take the responsibility for finding out what it is he really wants to do."

"I want to be a piano tuner," said Debbie. "And I want to be as good as my grandpa."

"Right now, you had better go home and put on a dress," Mr. Weinstock told her. "And don't stop to tune any more pianos on the way. Come straight back here, because we must have lunch in plenty of time before the concert."

"Wait until she hears you play!" he said to Isaac Lipman after he had helped Debbie on with her coat and hat and opened the front door for her. "And if that doesn't inspire her . . ."

"I think it *will* inspire her," chuckled Mr. Lipman. "I think it will inspire her to want to tune grand pianos for concert pianists."

Mr. Weinstock laughed. "If that's the case," he said, "then maybe I had better teach her how."

"Well, I think you should, Reuben. It seems to me she has a real talent for it."

"Yes, I was amazed at how well she was doing! But, you know, I wanted something better for her."

"What could be better than doing what you love?" asked Mr. Lipman.

. • .

At the concert, Debbie and Mr. Weinstock and Mr. and Mrs. Perlman sat in the first row of seats, a little bit over to the left, so they could watch Isaac Lipman's hands.

Everybody in town seemed to have heard that he had come, and all the seats in the Auditorium quickly filled with dressed-up and excited people, who rose to their feet, clapping and shouting "Bravo!" when the lights went down and the famous pianist walked out onto the stage.

He bowed to the audience and, sweeping back his long coattails, sat down at the piano. Everyone in the audience held his breath while Mr. Lipman sat with his head bowed and his hands in his lap. After he had raised them to the keyboard and begun to play the first piece on the program, a long fantasy and fugue by Bach, everyone began to breathe again.

They clapped loudly when it was over, and Mr. Lipman stood beside the grand piano and bowed. Then he swept back his coattails and sat down again, looking at his hands in his lap. The audience waited quietly, and he began to play a sonata in three movements by Beethoven.

At the end of the first movement, Mr. Perlman and Debbie clapped, but Mrs. Perlman and Mr. Weinstock did not. Debbie was amazed. "Didn't you think it was good?" she asked her grandfather.

"It isn't over yet," he said.

After the second movement no one clapped, but after the third, which was really the end of the piece, everyone clapped and shouted,

"Bravo! Bravo!" Mr. Lipman bowed and left the stage, but the clapping and calling continued until he came back to bow two more times. Then the lights came on, and everybody got up to walk around.

"That was good," said Debbie.

"You liked it!"

"Yes. No matter how hard he played, the piano stayed in tune. You did such a good job," said Debbie.

"It sounds as if you've got an assistant there, Mr. Weinstock," said Mr. Perlman.

"Sh-h," whispered Mrs. Perlman. "He doesn't want her to be a piano tuner! He wants her to be a pianist."

"What's wrong with being a—" began Mr. Perlman, but the lights started to dim, and everyone went back to their seats.

In the second half of the program, Isaac Lipman played two rhapsodies by Brahms, and *Carnaval*, by Schumann. At the end of the concert the audience clapped and clapped and called "Encore! Encore!" until he came out on the stage again and sat back down at the piano. He looked out at the audience and said, "A waltz by Chopin."

"Ah-h-h," said the audience.

They clapped and clapped when it was over. Mr. Lipman bowed and left the stage. The audience kept clapping, and he came back, bowed, and left the stage again. The audience kept on clapping until he came back and sat down at the piano again: "*Reverie*, by Mendelssohn."

"Oh-h-h," murmured the audience, and Isaac Lipman played the same piece Debbie had played that morning. After he finished, bowed, and left the stage, Mr. Weinstock, still clapping, said to Debbie, "Wouldn't you like to be able to play it like that?"

"No," said Debbie. "Grandpa Reuben—"

Mr. Lipman came back onto the center of the stage, bowed again and again, and went out. Then the lights came on in the Auditorium, and the concert was over.

"Grandpa Reuben, please let me be a piano tuner," said Debbie.

"We must go backstage and say goodbye to Mr. Lipman now," said Mr. Weinstock. "He will be leaving right away."

The whole audience was pushing backstage to shake hands with the great pianist. "Please, Grandpa Reuben," said Debbie. "Please teach me how to be a good piano tuner!"

"What's wrong with being a piano tuner?" asked Mr. Perlman. "Especially a good one!"

"Nothing," said Mr. Weinstock. "Debbie—"

They had come near Mr. Lipman by this time, and even though he was talking to some other people, he reached out and took Debbie by the hand. "You must come to the city and tune my piano sometime," he said.

"Yes, but first I am going to teach her how to do it," said Mr. Weinstock. "I was just about to say so."

Isaac Lipman was as delighted as Debbie. "So even after hearing one of my concerts, you would rather tune pianos than play them," he said. "Well, I was just like that at your age. I could only think of one thing. For me, of course, it was playing! When I get back to the city, Debbie, I am going to send you a leather bag of your own, filled with good tuning instruments."

"Thank you very much!" said Debbie. "And—"

"Yes?"

"And regulating tools, too, Mr. Lipman? Key pliers and bending pliers and a key spacer and parallel pliers and a capstan screw regulator and a capstan wrench and a spring adjusting hook and a spoon bending iron and—"

Some of the people who were standing near them were laughing.

"Everything!" cried Mr. Lipman. "I will ask the head of the piano factory for one of everything."

"Except the tools that I invented," put in Mr. Weinstock. "But I am going to make those for her, and she will be the only other piano tuner to have them."

Debbie put her hand into his. "I'll be just like you," she said.

Now early every morning Debbie Weinstock jumps quickly out of bed and runs downstairs to wash her face and brush her teeth at the kitchen sink. She puts water on to boil in the blue-and-white enameled saucepan and the old yellow coffeepot, and sets the table with the blue plate and the orange plate, the navy-blue bowl and the green bowl, the plaster salt and pepper shakers with seashells stuck into them and bright red plastic tops, the knives and spoons with yellow plastic handles, two white paper napkins, and two big white cups. Then she goes out into the hall to wake up her grandfather.

"Hm-m-m-m-m," she sings in front of his closed bedroom door. "Hm-m-m-m-m."

"Hm-m-m-m-m," comes Mr. Weinstock's voice on the exact same note. "Hm-m-m-m-m. I think we are both right this morning, Debbie."

She takes her shining new tuning fork out of its case, hits it against her knee, and holds it, singing, to her ear. "We *are* right, Grandpa Reuben!" she says, and goes upstairs to get dressed and make her bed while Mr. Weinstock is getting up.

# A Little Schubert

In a cold and snowy town called Vienna,
a short fat young man with a small round nose,
round eyeglasses, and curly hair
lived in a bare little room without a fire.

He was a composer.

Every morning he sat at a little table
and wrote music as fast as it came into his head.

Franz Schubert heard music
when his friends heard nothing,
and Franz Schubert heard music
that no one had ever heard before.

He heard so much music in his head
he could not possibly remember it all.

So Franz Schubert was very busy writing down his music
and he did not mind his bare room or his shabby clothes.

But when the cold made his fingers ache,
and he almost could not write his music,
Franz Schubert got up.

He clapped his hands
and stamped his feet.

He made his shabby coattails fly
as he danced to keep warm.

# Me and My Captain

There is a fishing boat anchored
on the windowsill below my shelf,
and I smell a briny smell
coming from it.

Looking down at its white cabin
with the green-painted roof
and bright red-colored flag,
I dream of her captain
coming up to see me.

He would notice at once
that I have a ship in a bottle
and a collection of seashells,
and ask me to marry him.
Then I would invite him
to stay for dinner.

One good thing about being a doll
is the food.
It is made out of plaster
and appetizingly painted,
so unless it gets too chipped or dusty
or left in the sunlight to fade,
it remains fresh-looking forever—
a feast for the eye.

If I were to serve the captain
with some,
and set the table with my Bristol dishes
and silver salt and pepper shakers,
he would really be amazed
at his good luck!

"Salt?" I would offer.
"What? An old salt like me?"
he would say back.
And I would laugh and laugh.

He would feed my dog scraps of food
under the table,
and we three would be so cozy together.

Since the captain of a fishing boat
is often gone on long voyages,
my dog and I would stay here,
and our life would be just the same
as before.

But we would have someone to watch for
and wait for
and hope for good weather for.

And whatever happened
while he was away
would be something to tell him about
when he returned.

Even without knowing him,
when I look down at the captain's boat
on the windowsill,
I feel happy because he is there.

# Fish for Supper

When my grandmother went fishing,
she would get up at five o'clock
in the morning
and make herself breakfast,
then clean up the dishes fast, fast,
and go down to the water
wearing her big sun hat.

With cans of worms and minnows,
some fruit for lunch,
bobbers, lines, hooks, and sinkers,
she rowed out in the rowboat
and stayed on the lake all day.

Over its sunlit waves and ripplets
she could see her yellow boathouse
staring back at her with dark eyes
from the shore,
while she waited for the fish to bite.

She caught sunfish, crappies, perch,
and sometimes a big northern pike.
When she came home in the evening,
she cleaned the fish
and fried them in butter.

She took fresh rolls out of the oven,
put water for tea on the stove,
and sat down and ate very slowly,
taking care not to choke on a bone.

Then fast, fast, she cleaned up the dishes
and went to bed,
so she could get up at five o'clock
in the morning
to go fishing.

# My Crazy Sister

# MY CRAZY SISTER

My sister came to live with me
and turned my whole house upside down.
She drove here in a car
loaded with everything she owned,
her "treasures," she told me.
I said to her, "You are *my* treasure."
After the excitement and confusion
of greeting each other
and bringing her things in from the car,
I put on the table a beautiful dinner,
"like magic," she said,
and we sat down to eat.
We hardly talked during the meal.
Later, with two pink desserts
and two good cups of tea,
for the first time we really looked at each other
and felt our deep joy in being together.
I looked around my room
and saw how her things fit in without crowding.
The car and TV were large and exciting,
but her other belongings were very small:
a wooden chair, a cradle.
"Sister," I said,
"those things look like they are for a baby."
"My baby!" she cried, staring around.
"You mean you have a baby?"

"I did, I did!" she moaned.
My crazy sister.
At last we found him high up on my shelf,
where she had placed him
between the clock and the vase.
Once he was safely down
and we fed him milk and a little cake,
my sister put him in his cradle.
There he lay calmly and caused no more worry.
What a good baby!
Without my even having to ask her,
my sister helped me clean up the kitchen.
Then we went out to the porch
and sat down on the glider
and watched some television before bed.
We turned a knob, and show people were in the room.
They talked.
We turned a knob, and they were gone.
Now there is such a feeling of happiness inside me
as I lie beside her in the semi-dark,
because there is a light on for the baby
that stays on all night.

## MY CRAZY SISTER
## BUYS A RAILROAD CAR

Soon after my sister and her baby
moved into my house with me,
we carried the washtub
in from the porch
and gave the baby a bath.
"Today is his birthday," my sister told me.
"Not really!" I cried.
"What would you like for your birthday?"
I asked the baby.
"Choo choo," he said.
And because it was a special day,
we put him in the middle of our big bed
for his nap.
Then I went to the door with my sister.
"Buy him a train," I whispered.
"I just hope I can find one," she said
as she got into her car and drove off.
I stayed home in the kitchen,
so even though the baby kept waking up
and I kept telling him,
"Sh-h! Go to sleep,"
by the time my sister came home,
his birthday cake was ready.
"Did you get it?" I whispered.
"Come out here and see," she said.

I went out the door in a hurry.
There stood a railway car in our yard!
"Sister," I said, "I meant a *toy* train."
"Did you?" she asked me.
My crazy sister.
The baby was up again when we came in,
and we carried his birthday dinner outside.
"Whoo-oo-whoo," said the baby
when he saw his amazing present.
"Whoo-oo-whooo"—just like a train whistle.
After dinner I had a surprise for my sister.
Back into the house I went
and got my guitar and banjo
from under the bed.
We put them around our necks
and tapped our toes and sang:
*"Freight train, freight train, goin' so fast,*
*Freight train, freight train, goin' so fast . . ."*
*"Whoo-oo-whooo,"* sang the baby.
*"Whoo-oo-whooo-oo-whooo-oo,"*
until it was late,
and we had to go inside
and go to bed.

# MY CRAZY SISTER
## STEALS AN AIRPLANE

To show my sister I was glad
that she and her baby lived here,
I bought her a picture of Amelia Earhart,
the great American woman flier.
She put it right up on the wall.
"Do you think I look like her?"
she asked me.
"A little bit," I said.
That night my sister rolled out of bed,
and the bump woke me up.
"Sister," I asked, "are you all right?"
"A-okay," she called from the floor.
"I just had to make a crash landing."
I told her she was only dreaming,
and she got back in bed.
But the next morning she acted very quiet,
and soon after breakfast
I heard her car drive away.
It was late afternoon,
and the baby and I were digging in the garden
when my crazy sister came home
dragging a small plane behind her car.
"Ah-h!" cried the baby.
"He remembers it," my sister said.
"We saw it standing in a cornfield

the first time we came here.
Now it's missing a propeller,
but I'll find one somewhere.
The pilot shouldn't have abandoned it,"
she added sternly.
Then we all admired the plane's straight wings
and its wheels and slender body
until the sky grew pitch-dark.
Back inside the kitchen with the lights on
I made popcorn in a pan.
Then the baby fell asleep,
and we put him to bed.
But at last we were too tired to go on talking
about the places we would see
when my sister learned to fly her plane.
No sooner had we gone to sleep
than we were both wide awake,
staring at each other under the blankets.
There were loud men's voices in our yard,
and we heard a great clanging and banging.
"The pilot and his mechanic!" breathed my sister.
In the morning when we went outside,
the little plane was gone.

# Family
# Scrapbook

# THE NIGHT WE GOT A PICKUP TRUCK

An unfamiliar horn kept beeping,
but I was standing on a busy corner,
looking for my father's car,
so at first I didn't see him
sitting behind the wheel
of a shiny blue pickup truck.
"Surprise!" he said to me.
"We traded our car in for this beauty,
right there on the used-car lot."
I got in beside my mother,
who took my brother on her lap,
and when we had to stop
in the heavy downtown traffic,
I felt glad to be sitting so high up.
"It seems safer than a car," said my mother.
"Oh, it *is*," my father said.
Fifteen minutes later, we were out of town,
and he pulled over to the side of the road.
"Who wants to ride in back?" he asked me.
"I do!" I cried.
Riding along under the sky
in the evening air,
as the countryside became more familiar
closer to home,
sitting alone on the floor of the truck,
I started to sing a camp song:

*"Te-ell me wh-hy the stars do shine,*
   *Te-ell me wh-hy the i-ivy twines . . ."*
Then, over the noise of the motor
   and the tires on the road,
   my mother joined in on a higher note,
   harmonizing with me:
*"Te-ell me wh-hy the sky's so blue,*
*And I will tell you just why I-I love you."*
Without saying anything,
   we took deep breaths
   and began again together,
   this time even sweeter than before:
*"Be-cause God ma-ade the stars to shine,*
*Be-cause God ma-ade the i-ivy twine,*
*Be-cause God ma-ade the sky so blue . . ."*
We rode into our driveway,
   my father stopped the truck,
   and in the silence we finished:
*"Be-cause God made you, that's why I-I love you."*
The grass, the trees, and our house
   all looked gray in the dark,
   and I saw my little brother sleeping
   when my parents opened their doors
   and the ceiling light came on.

# A SURPRISE FOR MY FATHER

One day, my mother and father
drove into town with my little brother.
I decided to stay at home
and practice the harmonica:
"*Wheee-whooo, wheee-whooo, heee-hoo, hee.*"
From my seat on the porch
I noticed a car
drive by on the highway,
and after a while it came back the other way,
slowed down, and turned into our driveway,
and a tall, handsome man got out.
I could see he was a pilot with a broken wing
—I mean, arm.
"Does the doctor live here?" he asked me.
When I said yes, he nodded to the driver,
who waved at him and rode away.
"Please come in," I said.
"My father will be back soon."
"Oh, I hope so," he groaned.
Then he lowered himself into the swing
and shut his eyes,
and I could see that he was in pain.
As soon as he opened them again,
he noticed my harmonica
on the windowsill.
"Do you know 'The Handsome Young Airman'?"

he asked me.
"Well, you're—" I began bashfully.
But he had raised his chin,
fixed his eyes on the rafters,
and in a pleasant voice started to sing:
*"A handsome young airman lay dying,*
*And as on the airdrome he lay,*
*To mechanics who 'round him came sighing,*
*These last parting words he did say:*
*'Take the cylinders out of my kidneys,*
*The connecting rods out of my brain,*
*The crankshaft out of my backbone,*
*And assemble the engine again.'"*
"Oh!" I said when he was done.
"My father would really love that song.
He was a doctor in the Air Force
when I was born."
The pilot threw his good arm across his eyes
and astonished me by saying,
"You *look* like your father! Sawbones Frankel!
We were in the service together."
"You were?" I exclaimed.
"Sure. I'm still flying—I'm a crop duster.
Gosh, it'll be good to see him again."

# MY BIRTHDAY

On the morning of my birthday,
my parents and little brother kissed me.
They sang "Happy Birthday,"
and when I picked up my napkin,
I found money.
They cried, "That's for a present
from town this afternoon!"
My mother helped me clean my room,
then I held my purse in my lap
on the ride into town.
"Aren't you coming?" I asked my father
when he finally stopped the car.
But he told me to have a good time,
and he'd meet me there at three.
"If I get paints, I'll be an artist,
if I get a book, I'll be an author,
if I get clothes,
I'll be a dress designer," I said,
taking long steps down the street.
I stopped in front of the drugstore.
They had cameras in the window!
I made up my mind and went inside.
I came out into the sunlight
carrying a square black camera
by its neat little handle,
and I had the instruction folder

and an extra roll of film in my purse.
I walked along like a photographer,
staring hard at everything,
wondering if I should take a picture.
When I felt hungry,
I went into the dime store
and sat down at the lunch counter.
I ate my chiliburger slowly,
thinking about the pictures I would take:
the popcorn wagon
that parked near my school sometimes,
and the sun inside our kitchen,
every summer afternoon,
lighting up the sink.
After I paid, I went to the park
and practiced looking at trees
through the viewer.
"So that's what you see," I said to my camera,
because we were partners.
I took a picture of the library
and heard my camera's nice, loud click.
On the way to meet my father,
I vowed to take it everywhere.
"It will be my constant companion," I told him.

# YOM KIPPUR

On the Jewish High Holy Day,
Yom Kippur,
neither my little brother nor I
went to school.
We put on our best clothes
early in the morning,
and I whispered to my brother,
"Be careful when you brush your teeth
not to swallow any water!"
But my mother told me,
"Children don't have to fast all day,"
and she gave us milk and cereal.
Our temple was sixty miles away.
My father drove us there in time
to hear the organ play,
before the rabbi rose and said,
"This is the day of God."
We read the prayer Aveenu Malkaynu:
*"Our Father, our King, we have sinned before Thee.*
*Our Father, our King, inscribe us for blessing*
*in the book of life.*
*Our Father, our King, grant us a year of happiness . . ."*
When the morning service was over,
our family walked in the park
and picked up colored autumn leaves.
"I'm hungry," said my brother.

In temple again, we stood and exclaimed,
"Let us adore the ever-living God,
and render praise unto Him
who spread out the heavens
and established the earth . . ."
During the rest of the afternoon service,
I looked at the leaves in my prayer book.
My brother slept on my father's arm,
and every time we had to stand,
my father gently moved him over.
Suddenly the shofar blew:
*"Te-keeeeeee-ah!"*
"Good Yontif!" cried my mother.
Everyone shook hands with the rabbi,
and it was dark when we went out
into the cold air.
We ate at a drive-in on the highway.
My mother said, "We should have a feast,
after praying and fasting all day."
"This seems like one," joked my father.
But after we got home that night,
we sat at the clean kitchen table together
and had apple slices dipped in honey,
"for a sweet year."

# OUR FRIEND MR. JOHNSON

From the earliest time I can remember,
my father kept on his desktop
two round seashells called cowries.
The brown-spotted tiger cowrie
had a thin yellow stripe down its back,
and the golden cowrie's back
was a deep, shining orange.
First I, and then my brother,
when he got older,
could carefully play with them
on the floor in front of the oil burner.
This is how we played:
One day the two cowries went for a walk.
Suddenly the tiger cowrie turned on his side
and showed his teeth to his friend.
The golden cowrie turned on *his* side
and showed *his* teeth!
Then they continued their walk
all around the oil burner,
one in each hand of my little brother.
Sometimes in the evening after supper
my father picked up his guitar
and began strumming.
Then our neighbor Mr. Johnson,
an old black man
who had arthritis in his hands,

would always hear him and come over.
He couldn't play anymore,
but he taught my father some new songs,
like "Crash on the Highway"
and "The Great Speckled Bird,"
and said that he was getting good.
One night while we were all singing
and Mr. Johnson was stamping his feet,
my brother got so carried away
he started to hit the cowries together.
"Stop!" cried my father. "They'll chip!"
I hurried to the kitchen,
where my mother was working,
and brought back a pot and its lid.
"Now you have a drum," I told him,
but the noise he made with them was deafening,
and our friend, Mr. Johnson, went home.
The next day he returned,
bringing a real African drum.
It had a sweet, small, wild sound,
and my brother played it very rhythmically.
"Thank Mr. Johnson," my father told him.
*Tip! Tip! Tap! Tap!*
"You're very welcome," said Mr. Johnson.

# NEW YEAR'S EVE

My mother went to the beauty shop
on the morning of New Year's Eve,
and when she came home,
not only was her hair curled,
but the top wave was sprayed gold,
and the rest sparkled
with silver sprinkles!
All day it looked strange
with her housedress and apron.
But after my father came home
and we had dinner,
my little brother and I helped her
do the dishes.
Then she went upstairs
to put on her green taffeta dress,
matching shoes, and pearl jewelry,
so everything was beautiful together.
"How do I look?" asked my father,
to tease her.
"Wonderful!" we shouted.
"Here are some snacks for you,
and this is the telephone number.
Take good care of each other,"
my mother said to us before they left.
First we shared a can of Vienna sausages,
then we listened to the radio.

Next we played some card games.
"Will you tell me a story?"
my brother asked me.
I sat down on the couch beside him
and, in my scariest voice, said,
"It was a *cold* wintry night.
Three thieves sat around the fire.
'Pete,' said the chief, 'tell us a story.'
'Oak,' said Pete, and the story began:
It was a *cold* wintry night.
Three thieves sat around the fire.
'Pete,' said the chief, 'tell us a story.'
'Oak,' said Pete, and the story began:
It was a *cold* wintry night."
(My brother started laughing.)
"Three thieves sat around the fire.
'Pete,' said the chief—"
Just then we heard the front door open
and felt a cold, perfumed wind
as our parents came in!
"Good, you're up!" cried my mother gaily.
"Dad and I left the party early
so we could be with our sweethearts
to welcome in the New Year."

## ALBERTO GIACOMETTI

Sitting on our porch,
I read from a magazine
how inside Paris,
a bright and dreamy city,
there lived a man
named Giacometti.
His hair looked gray
and his clothes and hands were gray
from working in a studio
where even the daylight
streamed in gray.
Its walls were gray,
his pencils, brushes, benches,
bottles, tools were gray,
and everyone who went to see him
came out covered with the dust
of clay and plaster,
because he was a sculptor.
Giacometti worked hard,
slapping heavy handfuls of wet clay
onto an armature.
Then, dancing around it
like a fighter,
gouging it and scraping it
to make a figure,
he took so much away

it seemed to cry,
"What is man but dust?"
And gasping with despair,
Giacometti swore
that he couldn't create
a single thing he saw.
He also was a painter,
digging long, narrow brushes
into colors of clay.
His canvas on an easel,
he painted in with white and black
and painted out with gray.
He painted in with white and black
and painted out with gray.
Nobody asked him to do it,
and only he cared if he stopped.
He was an artist.
"What is man but dust?"
Giacometti seemed to ask
as a tall, thin plaster figure
was borne out of his gray studio
for casting into bronze.
And the answer came back:
"Glory!"

# My Noah's Ark

When I was a little girl,
ninety years ago,
my father made me an ark.

And I know he had fun
building it,
because once I heard his voice
behind a closed door,
booming like God's:
"Make it three hundred cubits long."

The Noah he carved
had a hammer in one hand
and a mop in the other,
and Mrs. Noah carried a saw.

Two spotted leopards,
two meek sheep,
two gray horses,
and two white doves
were already in their compartments
in the ark
when my father gave it to me.

The smaller gray horse looked sad,
and I always stroked her

with my finger,
until to this day
there is not much paint left on her,
except for her two little eyes,
which look grateful.

Over the years, as I grew up,
my father added more animals:
a pair of brown bears,
a bull and a cow,
a hen and a rooster,
two striped tigers—
and oh, I enjoyed playing with them!

When I got married,
my husband teased me.
But I remember how gently
he carried the ark
to my new home.

I taught our children
the story of Noah,
and how their grandfather shouted
behind a closed door:
"Make it three hundred cubits long."

Now everyone is gone,
and the ark holds their memories.

Our fun and sorrow
seem to form a rainbow,
and it warms me
like sunshine.

# Natural History

Our planet is a lively ball
in the universe.
Oceans move ceaselessly,
and below, in the deep,
fish swim, mollusks hop,
and plants wave silently.
Tiny grains of sand
keep the powerful waters
from flooding lands
where trees grow skyward.
It looks so peaceful
from afar.

But little puffs of smoke
erupt
where men are fighting,
or shooting ducks down from the sky,
or breaking mountains.
Homeless dogs and cats
are scared and lonely.
Old people look in garbage
hopefully,
though we have riches
we are born to share.

Low trees hold fruit
and vegetables lie warmly
in the dirt
or hide on vines.
Waves of wheat and corn
shimmer in the sun.
They are made for people.
They're made for cows
who nurse their calves.
They're made for gray wolves
with their pups.
They're made for ducks
and singing birds and snakes
and little minks.
Every living creature
is our brother and our sister,
dearer than the jewels
at the center of the earth.

So let us be
like tiny grains of sand,
and protect all life
from fear and suffering!

Then, when the stars shine,
we can sleep in peace,
with the moon
as our quiet night-light.

# Neighbors

# NEIGHBORS IN AUTUMN

The first time I saw
my new neighbor,
she was waving goodbye
to her moving van.
I ducked back inside my house
to take a sponge bath
and change my kerchief
before going over there.

Then, on my way out the door,
I thought,
"I ought to bring her a pie!"
I'd never baked before,
but I had some recipes.

And following directions,
I rolled out the dough.
I rolled out the dough,
I rolled out the dough.
I sneaked out my back door
and ran to the grocer's
to buy more flour
and sugar and butter.
Back home again,
I rolled out the dough
and rolled out the dough.

Late that afternoon,
I took a hot, crispy pie
out of the oven.

I removed my apron,
covered up the pie
with a clean napkin,
and went through the leaves
to my neighbor's house
and rang the bell.
"Welcome," I told her.
"Please come in!" she cried.

I sat down on a crate
and tried to stay awake.
Suddenly it was evening,
and she had just finished
hanging up her curtains.
"Everything looks lovely!"
I said.

# NEIGHBORS IN WINTER

When I saw my new neighbor
out shoveling snow,
I ran into the hallway
and pulled on my boots,
got into my overcoat,
found mittens,
took my shovel,
and went outdoors,
into the icy blast.

My neighbor was halfway down
her front walk by then,
heaping thick shovelfuls of snow
left and right as she went.
I wanted to catch up with her.
"I'll just clear a small path,"
I declared.

But over the drifts
between our two houses,
I saw her shoveled sidewalk,
wide and clean and wet.
"Hi!" I shouted,
but she couldn't hear me.

"We'll meet each other
when she comes back," I thought,
then bent over
and began to work:
Scrape, throw!
Scrape, throw!

When I looked again,
her entire walk was clean
and starting to dry.
She had gone in.
I wanted to quit then—
I felt so alone.

At last I was done.
My eyes were blurry,
my cheeks stung,
my ears rang,
my fingers were numb,
and my toes ached.
Sitting inside my warm kitchen,
I wondered what my neighbor was doing.

# NEIGHBORS IN SPRING

I wanted to invite
my new neighbor over.
"But first," I thought,
"I'd better clean up."
And I took my socks off the chair,
and put them in the hamper.

I changed my bedsheets,
lemon-oiled the wood furniture,
and hit the cushions
against my knees.
Then I vacuumed everywhere:
Fffft! Fffft! Fffft!
I heard little bits of dirt
click inside the hose.

I washed and waxed my floors.
While they were drying,
I scrubbed out the bathroom
with a powerful cleanser.
I washed my china dog,
china house,
and china rabbit sisters
in hot, soapy water.
When they had air-dried,
I set them back

on my gleaming knickknack shelf.
I washed my mirrors,
the glass over my pictures,
and all the windows.

After I scoured the kitchen,
and climbed up on a stool
with a magazine,
I heard the doorbell ringing.
"Who is it?" I called.
"I brought you some lilacs,"
 said my neighbor.

"Thank you!" I cried.
"Don't mind the mess.
 I'm just cleaning house."
 My neighbor looked everywhere.
"What's there to clean?"
 she asked me.

# NEIGHBORS IN SUMMER

Standing outside my door
one morning,
looking in my neighbor's yard,
I saw four small bowls
left on her lawn,
one at each corner of the garden.

After some thought,
I went over
and picked them up,
spilled out the water,
then brought them to her door
and knocked.
"Are these yours?" I asked her.
"They're for the rabbits,"
said my neighbor.

"They'd dig up my vegetables,
because they want water."
"I never heard that before!"
I exclaimed.
Together we put the bowls back
and filled them from her hose.
"Please stay for breakfast,"
said my neighbor.

The inside of her house
was interesting.
Everything was different from mine.
What pretty dishes!
What soft chairs!
What a beautiful rug!
What shiny spoons!

"We have the exact same sugar bowl,"
I called to her at the stove.
"I'm so glad we're neighbors,"
she said, sitting down.
"It was hard moving in,
and I spent a lonely year."
"Next winter," I said quickly,
"after we shovel our walks,
let's have cocoa together
at one of our houses."
"Let's take turns,"
said my neighbor.

# Laughing Latkes

On Hanukkah,
the dreidels dance
because we spin them
to win
every nut and raisin.

But why
for eight nights,
in the candlelight,
are the latkes laughing?

That is a question
worth answering.

Does a latke laugh
for joy
because our temple
in Jerusalem
was not destroyed?

Do they
celebrate the might
of Judah Maccabee?
Do they picture
in Israel,
two thousand years later,

former prime minister
Golda Meir
also frying latkes?

Does a latke
laugh with pleasure
when children get
new books as presents?

Or does it make
a latke laugh
how each child thinks
his mother
can make latkes best,
with crisper edges
and more tender middles?

Do the latkes laugh
at sour cream
in borscht?
Do they laugh
when we put sour cream
on them?

On Hanukkah, we eat until
we can't spin a dreidel.

Do the latkes
laugh at that?

They're laughing
because they're potatoes!

# An Artist

*Only painting counts.*

—PISSARRO

An artist is like God,
but small.
He can't see out
of God's creation,
for it includes him.

With the seas divided,
all the animals named,
and the sun and moon
and stars
set in their tracks,
an artist spends his life
not only wondering,
but wanting to work
like God
with what he can command:
his paints.

He tries to copy
God's creations.

He tries to shape beauty
with his hand.

He tries to make order
out of nature.

He tries to paint
the thoughts and feelings
in his mind.

An artist is like God
as God created him.

Small, strong,
and with limited days,
his gift of breath
is spent
over his paint box.

Choosing and brushing
his colors,
he tries
to make paint sing.

# Lives of
# the Artists

# REMBRANDT VAN RIJN

*1606–1669*

Artists,
whether great or small,
give away their beauty,
and crave the work
of other minds
to feed their hungry eyes.
The greatest artist
of them all
was Rembrandt.
He had the largest appetite
for works of every kind.
One small tin pot
told him,
"You are not alone.
I am humble, too."
Twenty marble heads
of Roman emperors said,
"Once we were great
like you."
"You can be like us,"
said the paintings.
Two exclaimed,
"Raphael will never die
as long as we survive!"
"We seem to be miracles,
yet we led simple lives,"

said the seashells.
And the ancient weapons
and wind instruments
sighed,
"All land and sea creatures
lead simple lives
of great mystery."
One large mirror
silently agreed,
in Rembrandt's home
in Amsterdam.
Every outside
has an inside,
and every inside
has an outside.
Just one stroke
of Rembrandt's
chalk,
needle, brush, or pen
could tell both tales.
They tell them
to this day.

# FRANCESCO GUARDI

*1712–1793*

Guardi,
we don't know
too much about you.
Your sister wed
Tiepolo.
Your father,
your two brothers,
and your sons
were painters, too.
In your own time
Canaletto
was acknowledged as master
of the Venetian view.
Canaletto
stood on the Rialto,
looking at the houses
through a camera obscura.
He drew them in perspective
with a compass
and a ruler.
His highways of green water
and their reflective twin,
the skies,
were brushed dramatically.
That was not true of you,
Guardi.

Rows of buildings
on the lagoon
seemed to dance
before your eyes,
and their balcony railings
looked like the notes
to tunes
that flew away
from music paper.
Venice was made
on mushy land.
Laws changed,
and people died.
Guardi,
you must have dreamed
about the sky,
where order reigned.
Every little faraway cloud
you painted
has stronger architecture
than any home
on the canal.

# VINCENT VAN GOGH

*1853—1890*

Respect the speckled things
in nature:
the freckled arm
beneath the surgeon's
short-sleeved gown,
the eggs of birds,
their fuzzy young,
and the Dutch painter
Vincent van Gogh,
red, rough, gruff,
yet very tender.
The green caterpillar
he returned to a tree
did not hurt him, either,
nor the starving dog
he fed.
But he was hurt
by people.
And like the combination
of oil and turpentine
painters use,
he too
was a dangerous mixture
that might craze or crack.
He tried to stay away
from people,

even from his brother
Theo.
Lonely, ill, and poor,
he seemed to be
accursed in every way.
But was his misery
like dust,
purposely kicked up
to keep all jealous eyes
from his brushstrokes
of whirling beauty?
He rarely signed his art.
He once said,
"They will surely recognize my work
later on,
and write about me
when I'm dead and gone."
Harsh, rejoicing lines
of arm or leaf or stem
signify
that they were made
by Vincent's hand.

# PIERRE BONNARD

*1867–1947*


I did not go to Le Cannet
and climb the steps
to "Le Bosquet,"
where Bonnard lived
with his dachshund,
Poucette,
and the lady who liked
to take baths,
but I've been there.
The luncheon table
is always set,
and the clean lady sits still
in her chair,
red hair bent over
the dog's red fur,
above the white cloth
where the wine bottle stands,
and grapes and cheese—
I can see them.
The golden sun and the trees
and vines,
trying hard to get inside,
press themselves flat
at the windows.
Scratch, scratch, scratch,
Bonnard made notes

in pencil, on paper.
Later, alone
in his small gray room,
he painted those things
he saw every day
and loved to remember.
Around and around
went Bonnard's brush,
touching oil paint
to his canvas.
Around and around
went Bonnard's brush,
dipped in one color,
then another and another—
until the scene
seemed to be reflected
in a silver candy wrapper.
This is the way
the tall, thin, shy man
has invited us in.
Though he has gone,
we can stay there.

# LOUISE NEVELSON

*1899—1988*

Louise Nevelson
took a shipbuilder's name,
and the things she made
are seaworthy.
The wooden refuse
of New York City's streets,
of the sea,
lumberyard scraps,
and lathe-turned products
were gathered up by her
and taken home
and painted black as tar.
Years or days later,
or right away,
with a practiced hand
and eye,
they're placed
inside black boxes.
The quiet talk
among the black forms
in each black box
is never-ending.
They are radio receivers
of silence.
Louise Nevelson
wore beautiful clothes:

an early American quilt
made into a skirt,
a denim shirt,
and an emperor's robe
for work or sleeping.
Box upon box
she stacked into walls—
not only black,
but white or gold,
or clear or steel!
Why are the black boxes
whispering?
Of what do the white boxes
sing?
And the golden boxes
proclaim what?
Freedom, equality,
wastefulness, beauty.
Something American!
Leah Berliawsky
sailed to America,
and created American art.

# JOHANNES VERMEER

*1632–1675*

When you know it,
the sound of his name
strikes a golden tone:
Vermeer.
He lived in Delft,
a place made magic
by his own view
of a red, yellow, blue town
crusted with sugar,
pearls, or salt,
which no rainy gray cloud
could ever dissolve.
Closer at hand,
in *The Little Street*,
as each red brick
has its own place,
and each old woman
her job to do well,
the colored brushstrokes
of Vermeer
build a solid world
that is spacious,
light-filled,
calm, and beautiful.
Delft was known
for blue-and-white pottery—

tiles and dishware.
From Gouda came cheese
and Catharina Bolnes,
Vermeer's wife.
Of eleven children,
did the six daughters
model for their father?
We see girls
with their features
on the streets of New York.
Are they descendants
of Vermeer?
His thirty-five or so
known pictures
are like patterns
in the Oriental rugs
he painted, new and nappy
at that time,
with haloed dust specks.
The more worn they are,
the clearer they become.

# EUGÈNE BOUDIN

*1824–1898*

In an auction room,
a circle cut
in the stage floor
turns
as the auctioneer calls out
the number of a "lot."
A wooden easel on it
rides around and stops.
It's holding a small painting.
Numbers bounce
about the room,
always going higher.
"Fair warning,"
calls the auctioneer,
and brings his gavel
down.
Someone lucky
owns the painting.
But what of the poor,
color-spotted soul,
the painter,
dead one hundred years?
Don't feel sorry for him—
he had all the fun.
Boudin
"must have been an angel,"

said Courbet,
"to know the skies
so well."
But he was something better.
He was the last
in a long line
of Norman sailors,
and he was bound to paint
their contemplation
of the sea and sky.
At work at the beach,
beneath an umbrella,
in a way, he was an angel.
He taught Claude Monet
to paint from nature.
Neither one
came from Heaven,
but from towns
ringed around
with white canvas wings:
the ports of Le Havre
and Honfleur.

# THE WOODLAND INDIANS

I photographed
this Woodland Indian doll
very fast
through a glass
in a place
I don't recall.
You can see the beads
I wore
reflected at the upper left,
and that white line's
my camera chain
mirrored
on her friendly face.
For many years
this portrait

has hung alone
above my desk,
and I often wonder,
what is that distortion
in the bottom right-hand
corner?
I remember her "seed beads"
as turquoise in color,
her blouse as indigo blue.
I know her hair
came from a horse.
Her shining eyes
are "pony beads."
Only her tanned skin
could have been made
before the Europeans came.
And look
at her crooked smile.
She's heard lies.
She's seen starvation.
She misses the herds
of buffalo
on the prairie.
She holds the soul
of the woman
who made her and said,
"Be happy!
Carry few possessions,
go lightly,
and look around
in wonder,
while on the earth
as its guest."

# PAUL CÈZANNE

*1839–1906*

A great painting
in a great museum,
regardless of its subject,
is a portrait
of the artist
who, like a child,
gave his whole heart
to the project,
and in the end
knew disappointment
when his skill
could not match his dream.
So he began again,
and he began again.
And he began again
until he could no longer
hold a brush.
A great painting
in a great museum,
regardless of the artist,
is a picture
of some time that's passed.
Cézanne set apples
on a plate,
arranged a napkin,
but he did not sit

and eat.
He stared, and thought,
and slowly painted
what he saw:
shreds of colored air.
But not at all calmly!
Feeling dizzy and sick,
his legs like jelly,
when he looked in the mirror,
he saw a stranger.
He had reason
to leave Paris,
to stay in his hometown,
Aix-en-Provence.
As he loved the mountain
Sainte-Victoire,
he endured the hatred
of his neighbors.
For beside the dream
in his own mind,
a great artist
dies a failure.

# CLAUDE MONET

*1840–1926*


In your straw hat,
white beard,
your tweed suit,
neat boots,
on the wooden bridge
above
the water lilies,
or before
the flower beds
at Giverny,
how we love you,
Claude Monet!
We guard your image
in our minds
the way the poet
Mallarmé
tightly held
the small painting
you gave him,
past Versailles,
past Chartres Cathedral,
through the fields,
in the train back to Paris
from your home.
Master of the sunny day,
of snow,

and locomotive smoke,
enveloped
in the scent
of turpentine and oil,
you demanded
that we see
both the pigment
and a flower,
in painted air
and painted water.
You gave artists
new faith
in their brushes, paints,
and rags.
Loving flowers, you gardened
water and land.
Above your round palette,
big and balanced
as a boat,
you might have been a frog
taking in the view
from a lily pad.

# SIMCHA SCHWARZ

*1900—1974*

"I saw a wonderful show
on Sunday."
"Tell me, what did you see?"
"*David and Goliath.*
It is set in modern times,
vanished modern times.
Like the days of the Bible,
those days won't return.
It takes place in Rumania,
in a small Jewish village,
a *shtetl.*"
"What happens?"
"A woman with a duck,
a *katschka,*
tells David's mother
the Philistines will attack.
David is a shepherd.
'*Davidl! Oy, Davidl!*'
She finds him in a meadow.
'My son, please don't fight.'
'*Shalom, Mama.*'
He gives her the lamb
who pulls on his leash,
crying, 'Maaa, maaa.'
'*Hoy, Philishtine!*'
David comes to their camp.

A Philistine girl
dances before him.
She is thrilled by battle.
'Mm-m! Soldiers!'
David says he
will fight the giant,
Goliath.
Goliath calls for vodka.
David plays on his harp
and sings to the stars.
While he sleeps
Mother Rachel visits him
and brings him a stone.
The cocks crow.
David knocks out Goliath.
*'Eins! Zvei! Dre!'*
counts the referee.
So let there be peace,
*ʒoll ʒein shalom.*"
"These were puppets?"
"Yes, at the Hakl-Bakl Theater on
Rue Guy Patin."

# WINSLOW HOMER

*1836–1910*

*Oh, I'm not a king,*
*but I have a throne.*
*It's a high, smooth, flat stone*
*by the sea.*
*Clean and sunny,*
*cool and salty,*
*it is the stone for me.*
*I like to watch the boats*
*come in.*
*My father is on one of them—*
*my father and my uncle.*
*Sometimes my cousin*
*sits with me,*
*and as we look*
*at the sea,*
*we know that's where we'll be*
*someday,*
*when school is over.*
*Along comes a man*
*named Winslow Homer.*
*He's wearing a suit*
*and a straw boater,*
*and carrying a cane.*
*No, it's an umbrella!*
*He's got a box of colors*
*and a sheet of paper.*

*"Stay right there," he calls.*
*"What?" asks my cousin,*
*politely leaning down.*
*"I said don't move!"*
*Homer barks.*
*He's a famous artist*
*from Boston and New York.*

Americans
gaze out to sea,
homesick for the lands
from which we came.
Deafening, frightening, rolling,
eternal curve,
which broke
and shifted the continents
apart:
Winslow Homer was your neighbor.
He painted you at work,
minute and mighty.
He liked you best
when you were angry!

# CAMILLE PISSARRO

*1830—1903*

He was like the Good Lord
said the painter
Cézanne
and everyone liked
to go painting
with him.
He saw the seeds
and helped talent grow
in all his friends.
Can any raindrop say
of any flower,
I made this bloom?
Pissarro's touch
was like the rain.
The paintings he left
are natural.
They don't call out
his name.
But to his wife
he seemed as
terrible
as the eye
of a West Indian
hurricane
for he frequently said
that only painting
mattered.

They had two daughters
and five sons,
five sons,
all painters.
He wanted them
to be happy men,
neither rich
nor famous.
They followed him
and for a time
he followed them
for he was
a young old man,
fair-minded
as a sunny day,
at home
in a world
that was hard
on him,
content to paint
in all weathers.

# BERTHE MORISOT

*1841–1895*

Sometimes
I dream of the life
of the painter
Berthe Morisot,
whose mother complained
to her and her sister
about their messy studio.
The two sisters disdained
their drawing master,
and painted outdoors
with Papa Corot.
Both had pictures accepted
by the Salon,
where they laughed with
Manet
and all the great painters
of their day.
In the dark part
of the fairy tale,
sister Edma married
a naval officer.
The new Mme Pontillon
moved away from Paris,
leaving Berthe alone.
Berthe's brushstrokes
slashed and shimmered.

She was tense
as she hiked up hillsides,
looking for sites
to set up her easel,
in an elegant dress.
When she exhibited
with the Impressionists,
Monet, Pissarro, Sisley, etc.,
the newspaper *Le Figaro*
called them "lunatics,"
and went on:
"As in all famous gangs,
there is also a woman—
Mlle Morisot."
She married Manet's brother,
and had a daughter,
her favorite model, Julie.
Like all the gang's,
her paintings now hang
in the Louvre.
And so I dream
about her.

# EUGÈNE ATGET

*1857–1927*

Smell the white vinegar
in which in hottest water
he might have wrung a cloth
and wiped
from the wooden case
of his great camera
dust
of the early morning roads
around Paris.
To our eyes, his photos
have the same
plain, strong aroma.
In the streets,
he photographed vendors
as one to another.
His own customers
stayed at home.
Painters and historians
bought the pictures
he brought
in his old black coat
to their doors.
Those who knew him wrote
that he had strong opinions,
would only eat,
for instance,

milk and bread and sugar.
He did not want more
than he could afford.
He would not borrow
a smaller camera.
"It can photograph faster
than I can think,"
he said.
Though the gear he carried
weighed fifty pounds,
Mme Atget could print
the big glass negatives
by watching them lie
in wooden frames
on the terrace,
in the sun.

When she had gone,
he, too, was old.
"Come quick! I'm dying!"
he cried out.
He would have liked
to stay on.

# HENRI MATISSE

*1869–1954*

His squeaking charcoal
leaned around
the contours of a face,
and tiny wakes of soot
shot out
a fraction of an inch,
and slowly sifted
down the paper
to his knees.
His steely pen point,
dragged and drawn along
the outline of a leaf,
split apart and came together,
set off little storms
of spatters,
but his blue eyes
stayed fixed on his model.
He could trust his hand.
He did not mind the time
and space
his genius required.
It was like
a tropical plant
whose baby leaves
unfurl
and grow big as platters

on lengthening stems.
In his long white coat,
Matisse
transplanted his workshop
from Paris
to the South of France,
where palm trees sway,
to the Cimiez district
of Nice.
Still standing there
is his striped armchair.
How many models sat upon it
knee to knee with the "Doctor,"
who held a small white dish
in one hand
on which were squeezed
his colors?
He did not mind variety,
nor count how many times
he saw the same thing
differently.

# PIET MONDRIAN

*1872–1944*

We all rejoice
in the circle,
the wheel,
but who invented
the square?
I know who
would have liked to meet
him or her,
for he loved the right angle,
rectangle,
and plane.
When he was a young man,
Mondrian
drew trees
all the time:
their arching boughs,
muscular trunks and limbs,
the wet Dutch earth,
and sky.
He drew flowers
in their perfection
as all artists did
before him.
"But why copy nature
and paint an illusion?"
This stern man

who loved to dance
suddenly seemed to sing:
"Though God made heaven
and earth,
people invented geometry.
Curves close in
upon themselves—
straight lines extend
to infinity.
Light was a mystery
until Chevreul
invented
the color wheel."

Roads run straight
on a Mondrian.
Stop at intersections;
look around.
Fields of primary colors
contain every hue.
His paintings are plans
to refresh our minds.

# MARY CASSATT

*1844–1926*

Give me the life
of Mary Cassatt,
who went to
Paris, France,
to study art,
although her father said
he'd rather see her dead!
In her time
beauty and charm
were the two gifts
a woman must cultivate.
Strong enough
to choose not to marry,
Miss Cassatt
skipped charm and beauty
and concentrated
on her desire
to study the works
of great masters
in Italy, Holland,
and Spain.
She didn't skip romance,
though she met
Edgar Degas
in her studio,
not at a dance.

At once he proposed
that she exhibit
with the Impressionists.
"I accepted with joy,"
she said.
She etched and painted
mothers and children
while he attended
bathing women, the ballet,
the café, and the track.
He went with her
to the milliner
to watch her try on hats.
I am a bit
like Miss Cassatt.
I have the same
breed of tiny dog
who watches me draw,
and he doesn't know
I don't draw as well.
He's a Griffon
Bruxellois.

# MAURICE UTRILLO

*1883–1955*

Isn't it a great cliché
how the drunken son
of Bohemian artists,
up the garret stairs
from Paris,
in Montmartre,
painted scenes from postcards?
They hang in hotel rooms
where the lonely stranger,
gazing from his chair,
says, "I like that."
Utrillo's paintings
give us comfort.
The walls of Montmartre
are cracked, plastered,
peeling!
Behind each,
does someone sit
in quiet privacy?
Before each, people walk
independently.
You can hear their footsteps
ringing
in the narrow streets.
The skies are metallic;
the dead leaves
have fallen.

Small saplings stand
arrested,
their many-colored branches
frozen in the air,
saying, "We will wave
and we will bloom,
when you come home again."
His mother a hoyden,
his father unknown,
the streets of Montmartre
were home to Utrillo.
He was taken away,
and he drank.
Drunk, he was locked up.
But on the spot,
through photographs
or memory,
his brush tapped canvas,
and he was in Montmartre.

# MOSHE SAFDIE

*1938–*

If it's the shell
that curves the snail
and not the snail
that curves the shell,
as D'Arcy Thompson says
in *On Growth and Form*,
let's be careful
where we live.
Shall we become
flatheaded,
square,
unable to see
in all directions?
Oh yes, we will!

# Lives of
# the Artists

*Unfinished Fragments*

# PAUL GAUGUIN

*1848–1903*

A mandolin
hung on his wall;
he wore a sailor jacket;
he was small,
big bad Gauguin,
only five foot four.

# MARC CHAGALL

*1887–1985*

Who is that
leaning back
against the inside wall
of my filled water glass?
I mean
that dark-haired,
blue-clad angel
in bright armor
and folded wings.
I stand up
for just a minute;
now she's gone.

## HANIWA

Haniwa statue,
some old breath
is left in you,
and your hollow shell,
kept whole in museums,
is a hallowed container
of great dignity.

# A Writer

A writer
sits on her couch,
holding an idea,
until it's time
to set words
upon paper,
to cut, prune,
plan, and shape them.

She is a gardener,
never sure
of her ground,
or of which seeds
are rooting there.

She has grown
flowers, weeds,
a slender tree.
Now she dreams
of pansies
and heartsease.

At first daylight,
she sees
two small green leaves
close to the soil.

If a rabbit eats them,
she's not mad at him.
She knows more
will grow,
for a writer
always studies,
looks, and listens.

Thoughts that open
in her heart,
and weather every mood
and change of mind,
she will care for.

She's only one
of many writers,
working alone
at her desk,
hoping her books
will spread the seeds
of ideas.

# My Editor

This man
reads my work,
gnawing a cuticle.
Great! It's torn,
neat and clean.
He deserves this
quick success
in his work.

As he reads
my new book
in his cubicle,
I sit across
from his desk,
torn with love
I can't express,

because I'm not
the same person
who wrote
what he reads
with such great
yet divided attention.
At home alone,
sitting
on the couch
in my room,

staring into space,
I think
and erase,
think and erase.

This painful process
would rip a sheet
of paper,
but my mind
is thicker.

When I strike
something hard,
I keep calm,
saying it over,
cleaning it off.

I get up
to take a pen
and paper,
make each letter:
yes, those lines
of words are sound.

I'm an archaeologist
who's found her
site.

Day and night
I work hard
to rebuild
a little temple
no one knows
is there.

Lonesome
for my editor,
I call him
on the phone.

He used to say,
"Press on."
Now he says,
"Sounds good,"
or "Interesting,"
or "Hm."

Greatly encouraged
by this brush
with reality,
I begin to
hurry,
leaving some parts
buried,
and complete
my little structure
slightly
out of kilter.

I can't wait
until I shower,
dress,
chat with
a cab driver,
and deliver
my new book
to my editor!

He sees at once
where it's
missing
some stones.

"Oh, it's not,"
I assure him.
I don't want
to return
to the country
of origin.
"Think about it,"
he tells me.

I am thinking:
no one sought
this little temple;
now it's found,
leave it alone.

But he pokes here
and pushes there,
to see where
it caves in.

Sitting alone
at the desk
in my room,
I can't find
the buried words.
I try this;
I try that,
making lines up.

I try them
on my editor.
One, he says,
"locks into place."
I begin
to dig again,
and lose myself
in the excavation.

I remove
one big block.
Now only two lines
seem untrue.
"I'll get them,"
I tell him.

But my building
worries me.
It's stone-cold,
and I cry,
"Why not
have left it
wobbly?"

I tear it apart
and rebuild it
the old way.
Take it apart
and remake it
the new way.

Take it apart,
and suddenly see
how it goes.

"Why," my editor
  comically wonders,
"did this take you
  so long?"

Publication's
not the miracle,
but the friendship
of this man
for the me
I hardly know
but represent:
freshly showered,
in a plaid shirt,
trying to act
intelligent.

# Our Snowman

After our first big blizzard
at the start of November,
we had below-zero weather
and more snow fell every day.

Finally the sun came out.
The snow gleamed, heavy and sticky.

I zipped up my snowsuit in a hurry,
calling to my mother
to help get my little brother ready
to play out on our white lawn.

"The first thing we do," I told him,
"is build a snowman."

I patted a snowball between my mittens,
and when I squatted down
and started rolling it to show him how,
we were both surprised
at the quick way it picked up
a thick covering of snow.

Year after year, these things work!

"The important thing," I told him,
"is to roll it in fresh places,
 and not pick up mud or sticks."
He started rolling the bottom snowball
while I went away to roll the middle—
and way away to roll the head.

We hoisted our snowman together,
 and gave him a funny face.

Then my mother rapped on the window.
"Come in now," she called.

All during dinner I felt sad,
 because our snowman stood alone
 in the darkening night.

"We never should have made him,"
 I said to my brother.

Then I couldn't eat dessert.
"You're going to have a hard life
 if you cry over things like *that*,"
 my mother warned me.

But suddenly my father and I
 were dressing up warmly,
 and my mother turned the porch light on.
My father rolled the bottom and the middle,
 and I made the head.

I didn't dare tell *him*
 not to pick up dirt or leaves,

so the snowman's wife got full of them,
but it looked like a pretty gown.

When we came inside again,
my brother was glad for me.
"Now they each have company," he said.

# School of
# Names

I want to go
to the School of Names
to know every star
in the sky I can see
at night,
and later learn those
imagined
and proved to be there.

I want to know
what's in the ocean,
every school of fish,
every watery motion
by name.

I want to know
every stone and rock,
crystal, shale,
granite, chalk,
every kind by name.

Names of the continents,
names of the seas,
names of the islands,
names of the lakes,
names of the mountains,

names of shores,
names of deserts,
names of rivers,
and the grasses, flowers,
trees, and bushes
growing on this earth.

How are the winds called?

What are the names
of clouds?

I want to go
to the School of Names
to know everybody
with me
on this globe,
every mammal, reptile,
insect,
bird, fish, and worm.

I would like
to recognize
and greet everyone
by name.

For all the years
I may live,

no place but the earth
is my home.

# Artists' Helpers
# Enjoy
# the Evenings

I

Blanc, Noir, Gris, Bistre, and Sanguine were artists' helpers by trade, and good friends personally.

If they ever went to work in a desert, they swore they would not let go of Sanguine.

At dusk they held on to Gris, and at night, or working in muddy fields, they did the same for Noir and Bistre's sakes.

Through snow or fog, they made sure that Blanc did not disappear.

## II

When daylight failed at the artists' studio skylights, Blanc, Noir, Gris, Bistre, and Sanguine stopped working and went to a café.

Talk was loud and full of interest.

"Outlining," "highlighting," and "shading" were the words you heard, and sometimes they sang:

"We're slick and tall
Till the artists
Work us hard
And wear us down."

III

Gris's and Sanguine's families all did some work for artists.

The Sanguines lived quietly with their historic memories, but Gris came from a large, easygoing family, and both Blanc and Noir were related to them.

On Thursday evenings, Blanc, Noir, Bistre, and Sanguine went home with Gris for dinner.

These friendly evenings always made Bistre raise his glass and say, "It's hard living alone!"

IV

B lanc, Noir, Gris, Bistre, and Sanguine received their
invitations to the party of the year, the Artists' Helpers
Ball—a masquerade.

Carefully made up, they went as each other, fooled
everybody, danced every dance, and saw each other home
at dawn.

# Artists' Helpers Visit New York

I

Blanc, Noir, Gris, Bistre, and Sanguine, artists' helpers by trade, journeyed from Paris to New York by plane.

They left Charles de Gaulle Airport at ten a.m. and arrived at JFK at lunchtime, having gained six hours crossing the Atlantic.

They hoped to get green cards that would permit them to stay and work in the USA.

They were all looking forward to "le weekend."

## II

The walls of the five friends' motel room continually changed color as neon lights flashed outside in the street. While Gris and Sanguine wrote postcards to their families, Blanc, Noir, and Bistre tried all the TV channels.

Gris wrote, "The light here is great! The city is gray, but my pals don't have to hold on to me. There is color and light everywhere, day and night. We are going out to eat at a *diner*, where we listen to the *jukebox*."

## III

Using a map of their own making, Blanc, Noir, Gris, Bistre, and Sanguine went to visit the New York art stores.

They saw David Davis as they walked in his door. "Get green cards and get to work," he told them.

They went downtown to Pearl, came back uptown to Central, then went west to Torch before sliding into their favorite booth at the diner.

The American rock 'n' roll they had loved in Paris now made them homesick.

## IV

G reen cards for Blanc, Noir, Gris, Bistre, and
Sanguine arrived at their motel while they were
packing to return to Paris.

They packed their berets and wore new American
baseball caps.

They put the green cards in their wallets, saying, "These
will make fantastic souvenirs!"

# An Actor

"Good evening, ladies and gentlemen.
Welcome to my theater,
and to tonight's entertainment,
a playlet I have written
called *Porcelain Tea*.

From those same seats
you have wept for me
as a young prince
gravely wounded in battle,

anguished for me
as a senile king
who has been betrayed.

You have gazed with me
upon the world
with insane eyes
as, wearing flowers in my hair,
I went singing
to a watery grave.
You have laughed for me
as the mother
of mischievous twins,

and cheered me on
when, as a young queen,
I led
my battle-weary infantry.

Now I must go backstage
to my dressing room.
I will relax,
emptying my mind
of everyday thoughts
to prepare myself
for my role.

For when I return—
but *I* will not return—
it will not be me!

Thank you."

(INTERMISSION)

"Here is my doll,
Miss Porcelain Tea.

She has small seed pearls
for sugar lumps,
and an old rag doll
for company."

"Thank you. Thank you."

# A House,
# a Home

A house has skin
and eyes
and bone,
a head,
a breast,
a heart.

We move around
inside a house,
and look out through its eyes.

What the house sees,
we see.
What it feels,
we feel more gently.

Our backs grow against its steps.
Its porch welcomes sunlight
and offers shade.

Our jokes and songs
rise to its ceilings,
and rest beneath its roof.

We'll lovingly restore
its cracked and peeling paint,

lovingly replace
its broken windowpanes,
repair its frame,
mend its roof,
sweep its porch,
and warm its hearth.

Let the tunes fly!

# Sweet Sleep Canoe

Jump into
your sweet sleep canoe,
and gently ride
down the swiftly moving stream
of dreams.

High above you
in the sky
the moon
lights ripples
curling away
from your sweet bark canoe.

In your light canoe,
glide safely
down the swiftly moving stream
of dreams.

On either side
the grassy shores
brush past.
They're close enough to touch.
So rush peacefully
to dreaming.

Lie floating
in your sleek canoe.
Slide safely
on the swiftly moving stream
of dreams
until you arrive
with the lightening sky
at daybreak—
morning.

# PUBLISHER'S NOTE

M. B. GOFFSTEIN always wanted this collection of her picture-book texts—without the pictures. She once said it'd be like words without borders.

•

*Across the Sea* was originally published with two additional stories ("The Mill" and "A Little Squirrel Went Walking"). Brooke's manuscript for this collection omitted both stories, so they are not included.

*Sweet Sleep Canoe* was neither illustrated nor published. Brooke was unsure about including this unpublished text, but I've always loved the image in the title, so it's here.

•

"I like to write about artists," Brooke said in 1981. "Artists are people who are dedicated to something that's bigger than they are and every day is important to them because they can add to their work.

"*Lives of the Artists* is a book that I dreamed of doing from the time I started to write books. And I was amazed when I was able to achieve it. These aren't conventional biographies. They're distillations of the artists' lives and works. I read their lives over and over again until they became part of my own life and so in a way, I was writing out of my experience."

As Brooke prepared the manuscript for this edition, she wrote, "Some of the pieces I am including are fragments. Writing is never boring. You never learn how to do it."

•

The following were M. B. Goffstein's dedications in the first editions of these titles:

*The Gats!* to the memory of my grandmother, Fanny Rose Klapman

*Sleepy People* to my mother and father

*Brookie and Her Lamb* to my husband

*Across the Sea* to Grandma Rosie and the memory of Grandpa Nathan

*Goldie the Dollmaker* to my brother, Bob

*Two Piano Tuners* to my husband and our memory of Walter Hupfer

*A Little Schubert* to the Schaafs

*Me and My Captain* to Diane Wolkstein

*Fish for Supper* to the Goffsteins

*My Crazy Sister* to the memory of Melvin Loos, printer and teacher

*Family Scrapbook* to Michael di Capua

*My Noah's Ark* to my niece, Sarah Goffstein

*Natural History* to Barla

*Laughing Latkes* to Roz, Wally, Debby, Kathy, Andy, and Jill Bernheimer

*Lives of the Artists* to my parents, Esther and Albert Goffstein, and to David

*A Writer* to Charlotte Zolotow

*Our Snowman* to my niece and nephew, Sarah and Daniel Goffstein

*School of Names* to Antonia Market, Constance Fogler, and John Vitale—The Best!

*Artists' Helpers Enjoy the Evenings* to David

*An Actor* to Jackie Bartone

*A House, a Home* to David. Thanks always to Al Cetta, Melinda Joseph, and Al Eiseman and the printers at Eastern Press.

# ACKNOWLEDGMENTS

VERY SPECIAL THANKS to Brooke Koven for the
art and design direction and always being there.

THANKS TO EVERYONE at Girl Friday Productions,
especially the splendidly skilled and smart Karen McNally Upson,
for guiding this project through to its realization.

*Editorial:* Janice Lee and Amy Morby
*Design:* Rachel Marek